THE HORSE KNOWS

"These poems are delightful, with a fresh and original voice both in choice of subject matter and the treatment of topics. The poems are often witty, ironic, sometimes self-deprecating, with frequent original viewpoints and interesting imagery."
—*Tom Crawford, Retired Editor, Dover Publishing*

"Steve Swank sees the poetry in the ordinary gestures of life, and that's no small thing. The repairing of a chair, the perching of an eagle, some love, a little guilt, a creek behind the barn, and a lot of wondering—here they're all the stuff of poetry. Spend a little time with him. You won't be sorry."
—*Paul Negri, Former President and Publisher, Dover Publishing*

"Steve Swank, artist, poet, philosopher, jack of all trades, and fixer of all things broken, muses on the circle of life in this first book of poetry. His poetry expresses his mindfulness of his surroundings as he walks through town or down a country road or eats sushi with his son. It's contemplative, fanciful, and whimsical, and will appeal to all who wonder about their place in the vast universe."
—*Carol Karels, author of* Cooked: An Inner City Nursing Memoir, *winner of the American Journal of Nursing Book of the Year Award in 2005.*

"'Sometimes a poem can help to mend,' reads the opening of one of Steven Swank's charming meditations on the joys and aches of everyday existence. The claim may be a large one, but after reading this book, you may agree. Whether he's writing about taking out the garbage or awaiting a grown son's return from overseas, Swank projects a worldview that is as humorous as it is kindhearted."

—*Lucinda Rosenfeld, author of* What She Saw . . ., I'm So Happy for You, *and* The Pretty One.

THE HORSE KNOWS

Selected Poems

Steven Swank

Full Court Press
Englewood Cliffs, New Jersey

First Edition

Copyright © 2014 by Steven Swank

All rights reserved. No part of this book may be reproduced or transmitted in any form or by any means electronic or mechanical, including by photocopying, by recording, or by any information storage and retrieval system, without the express permission of the author and publisher, except where permitted by law.

Published in the United States of America
by Full Court Press, 601 Palisade Avenue
Englewood Cliffs, NJ 07632
www.fullcourtpressnj.com

Visit www.creativeimperatives.com
to see what else Steven Swank does,
or email him at sdswank@gmail.com

ISBN 978-1-938812-28-6
Library of Congress Control No. 2014931736

Editing and Book Design by Barry Sheinkopf
for Bookshapers (www.bookshapers.com)
Cover photo by the author
Author photo by Daryl Goldberg
Colophon by Liz Sedlack

Dedication

I dedicate this book to those human beings who forage and glean for self-knowledge. To those endeavoring to express themselves in ways peaceful and joyous toward their fellow human beings, I also dedicate this book. I salute and honor those attempting to live harmoniously with the other creatures dwelling on the water droplet we call Earth.

Acknowledgements

I wish to thank my wife Daryl Goldberg, and my family and friends, for their love, encouragement, and patience regarding my writing and the many other creative expressions of my life.

I thank my parents, Edith and Howard Swank, for teaching their children the importance of love and respect for each other, and for appreciating our place in the interdependence of all things.

I also thank my editor Barry Sheinkopf for his excellent understanding of the linguistic necessities of the English language. For his forthright critiques and helpful suggestions, I am most appreciative.

Table of Contents

As A Poet, *1*
Chance For Walt, *2*
This Little Poem, *3*
These Little Poems, *4*
Amish/English, *5*
You Must, *8*
Drumming, *9*
Fingers/Hands, *10*
Editor, *11*
Five-Inch Rain, *13*
As I Walk and Breathe, *14*
I Hoped, *15*
I Am Drawn, *16*
In The Attic, *17*
Men, *19*
Ironing A Fish, *20*
It's Just Math, *21*
Like Icarus, *23*
Maybe Today, *24*
My Fear, *25*
My Son Eats Fish, *26*
Friends Past And, *28*
On Another Day, *29*
The Waves, *30*
Solar Perplex-us, *31*
Sack of Hammers, *32*
Sometimes a Poem, *34*
Tender Shoots, *36*
The Boy, The Fish, The Brahms, *37*

The Chair, *39*
The Kitchen, *41*
The Little Bug, *42*
The Rivers Run Dry, *43*
The Snow, *44*
There, *45*
This Is Why, *46*
Asked, 48
You Said, *51*
Dear Friend, *52*
A Gift In All The World, *53*
Frost Is/You Matter, *54*
Alarms Will Sound, *55*
As My Son, *56*
Check the Rudder, *57*
Even In The Dark, *59*
Like Dogs, *60*
I Have Tools, *61*
At Arms' Length, *63*
What Do I Want?, *64*
I Watch You, *65*
Beneath The Snow Wait Seeds, *66*
The Horse Knows, *67*
How It Comes About, *68*
Rebecca A., *69*
Do You Know?, *70*
Mom Comes Home, *72*
Finding, *74*
Each Morning Now She Sits, *75*
Mom Is Angry, *76*
Bait on the Hook, *77*

Becca About Her Beau, *78*
Fixing, *79*
Elsewhere, *80*
Expect Sum Net Experiential Zen, *81*
Our New Mayor, *86*
Hear The Hum, *87*
How Good, *88*
How, *89*
I Bought Your Book, *90*
In Italy, *94*
Pencil Lead, *95*
City of Changes, *96*
You Surely Have, *97*
Little Bird, *98*
Love Magic, *99*
Predator Drones, *100*
This Poem, *101*
The Map Is Not The Territory, *102*
Busted Things, *104*
People Like You, *105*
Thoughts, *106*
Today Is, *108*
My Daughter Says, *109*
Well Intentioned, But, *110*
What When Walking We, *111*
Three Sides of the Circle, *112*
Poetry Suite, *113*
Why Men Never, *116*
Before The Sun Is Up, *117*
You Sparkle, *118*
In the Company of Angels, *119*

I Am, *120*
White Fluff, *121*
My Heart Is, *122*
Kite Tied to Toe, *123*
Puzzling It Out, *124*
He Says, She Says, *125*
A Vigil In Snow, *127*
But Words, *129*
Bring the Light, *131*
We Eat, *132*
It Is Not, *133*
Like Elephants, *134*
Life On The High Wire, *135*
The Tension, *136*

As A Poet

As a poet
I often have no income
but I am always working
in the realm of words,
the eye of an eagle,
the glistening trails of tiger snails
reflecting the inner architecture
of balance and tension
quietly like mirrors.

You are the polished surface
I can see myself in,
inverted in a spoon,
a store front window at noon.

I recognize
the symmetry of your laugh,
the view from your roof.

Chance For Walt

Behind the building
where trucks park
near the loading dock
in the pavement is a crack

This small opportunity
allows the rain to moisten soil
where a grass plant grows
five inches tall and blossoms.

This Little Poem

This little poem
is like a flower
that blooms in the desert
for about an hour.

These Little Poems

These little poems
like flakes of snow
have no weight

Even so they accumulate
and when you read them
they will melt

And there in time
tulips grow.

Amish/English

I live among the Amish;
as neighbors we love
and care for one another;
I borrow benches
for my wedding.

They call us their English,
and we call them our Amish.

Together we raise houses and barns,
together our children play,
together we celebrate and mourn
birth of a horse, a heifer, a child,
the passing of a loved one.

They call me their English,
and I call them my Amish.

I drive them to town,
they forge my steel,
we build community,
sharing a meal, lending a hand,
giving advice.
They are my Amish,
I am their English.

They allow me the honor
to nail the ridge board
while they hold support rafters
I wrap my legs 'round it
to keep from falling.

We are mutual,
we are friends.

I say I never met
an Amishman I didn't like;
they say I must not know
very many Amish,
which of course is true.

Our joy and laughter
sustain us during trouble.

A rush to the hospital
with an injured one
or sickness gives us
focus and empathy
as together we wait.

We share the fear,
we share the pain.

THE HORSE KNOWS

We bleed the same;
if our hand's in the saw,
the doctor says
how lucky we are
to still have fingers.

They make fun with my name
and well, it is funny, so I laugh.

You Must

You must envy, or I think you might,
those who manage to sleep all night.

Drumming

I think you might
like drumming, it is
delightfully expressive and primal. . .
like the beating of hearts,
rhythms flow
finding the pulse, celebrating life.

As the dancers on the floor,
so too our hands on the drum,
move fast, move slow. . .
or drag, then pounce
delicate like water
in a stony brook
or massive as
a grand cascade.

Fingers/Hands

My fingers won't open,
my hands don't close—
still they're useful,
a drummer knows,
for playing rhythms
on African drums.

I hope your fingers
are happy and free
to draw with crayons
some smiles from me.

Editor

He knows all the grammar:
why a smile is not a grin,
that a rhyme will need no hammer,
why some words go in the bin,
when to texture, when to smooth
what will trouble, what will soothe.

Or he finds some weird delight
in the past, a perfect tense,
and what modifiers might
help a phrase to uncripple
a way around the participle
if the sentence makes no sense.

Like a gypsy, do some telling
can you say, or let it slip,
how to value what I'm selling,
when will dock my wayward ship?
Could you offer just a clue
of the things you *wish* you knew?

When the cake has too much frosting,
what the national debt is costing,
when the tense I tend is tensing,
when the fence I mend is fencing,

must we always purchase guns
to protect our little ones?

Should the lion that is chasing
slow a bit for better pacing?
Can a pregnant pause be swelling?
From my bag of poor excuses
draw some reason for misuses
of the hyphen or the spelling.

When's reality not gestalt,
the pain I feel not my fault?
As the zipper teeth unjam,
will I remember who I am?
Can I use the courtesy turn
to full employ as I learn?

Five-Inch Rain

Yesterday, after a five-inch rain,
the creek, usually so demure,
thundered past the barn—
a roiling brown exuberance
carrying with it the smell of earth.
Heavy stones torn from their purchase
boom and bang in the roaring torrent.

Today, it is once again picturesque
with familiar clarity and babble;
the freshly scoured creek bed
smells of stone.

As I Walk and Breathe

As I walk the creek today
I trust my feet not to slip,
I trust my eyes will let them know
which stones will, or will not, tip

The farmhouse is most of two hundred years,
has knob-and-tube in the walls, floors that tilt,
a foundation of dry laid-up stone,
a ready source when it was built.

Sulfurous gas that is in the shale
works it way up through the well
from the faucet; if we choose;
we can ignite the eggy smell.

I Hoped

I hoped she forgot
but she remembers
so apparently not.

I Am Drawn

I am drawn
by complexity into hope
for a new adventure
with you.

I am drawn
by the sweeping click
of clock hands across
our space/time.

I am drawn
by the scent I imagine
we must express
together.

In The Attic

In the attic the sunrise blast pours
through the eastern window
as I sit at the roll-top desk
looking westward across the valley
of our small town.

Beyond are the Ramapo Mountains
so old as worn to bumps,
yet they gather first the light of dawn
looking far warmer than the frosted
terracotta rooftops nearby.

The birdbath, too, is frozen;
colorful leaves caught there
shine bright through the patterned ice
with marks a fern might make if bending down
during the night to kiss the surface.

A bald eagle has come to rest
in our neighbor's tree
to warm with grandeur, grace,
in silhouette imposing a silence
on the twittering birds.
Perhaps with a better idea in mind,
it leans forward,

casually pushing the earth away
as wings unfurl,
catching hold,
lifts in slow motion
for the rhythm of flight.

Men

In the rain
construction men
are looking down
a hole.

For one hour,
while getting wet
they point, and huh,
and jest.

Ironing A Fish

You might find it unlikely
and you may even doubt
but it isn't that easy
to iron a trout

but my wife said to me
as she ironed the fish
she won't serve it wrinkled
on the good china dish.

It's Just Math

Its just math
she says she teaches,
unremarkably. She muses,

It's just math
we must know for life
and understand some uses.

She wishes she had a special talent.
I say she has, it is so apparent;
to teach math, subtract and add,
to help protect our nation's youth
from the ravages of ignorance.

Math is such a vital subject;
teaching an enviable skill,
tenderly she engages children—
if they try, they know she will
help them achieve its mastery.

It is just math that allows our cars,
and our buses, to completely stop,
so our children arrive home safely.
My daughter runs
into the house yelling,

Daddy, today guess what,
I've learned some math,
like which is more, six times eight,
or nine times four! Oh, and why
the world keeps going round, and
how many ounces make a pound.

Could I dad, learn to cook?
I can read the fractions in our book
¼ this I understand,
and Dad please hand
me the measuring cup
so I can fill it halfway up.

When I rise to start my day,
the teacher has already taught
long division,
and when her day at last is done,
as she wipes the board,
if there be remainders,
she takes the fractions home,
planting them in clay pots,
whereby they grow up
to be whole numbers.

Like Icarus

Like Icarus,
if I had wings to fly
as high as I was able,
I would be looking
for someone like you.

Maybe Today

Maybe today I'll walk in the sun;
maybe today I'll get things done

Maybe today other things will matter;
maybe today my mind won't clatter
and bang, and clapper the bell.

My Fear

My fear is I will go someplace safe.
The name of that place is Not Caring,
where dreams sigh and dwindle.

I hope to find my balance soon
and be back in time for lunch
with energy enough to smile.

In the meantime, don't hesitate
to call if you must, but there is
no one to answer the phone.

Later I can tell,
I can listen,
hear and be heard.

How wonderful that sounds
to be forehead to forehead,
connect, and kindle.

My Son Eats Fish

My son eats fish at sushi bars
that arrive by train on little cars
that click and clatter slowly by.
He says, Hey, Pops, give this a try.
I close my eyes and wonder how
we've come to this from eating cow?

When I was a youngster, just a kid,
we went to basement freezer chest
where half a cow was lying at rest
with frozen squash, some lima beans,
and carrots were still considered greens.
Eating fish was not something we did.

It was a time before broccoli got invented;
we pounded out fenders if they got dented,
we changed our own oil, wore dungarees
with holes in the pockets and the knees.

He says, Pops, I know that's all true,
and here's more things you used to do—
you'd drink from the creek
where the cows had been pissing,
and drive to town
though a wheel was missing.

THE HORSE KNOWS

Hey, son, I begin to stammer,
don't make fun of my past;
your turn will come,
and pretty fast.

And so it went throughout the meal;
he ate the sushi with mustard eel
and I ate too, though not as much.
He promised to text and stay in touch.
I said, Please call, 'cause I don't text.
He called me old school, began to laugh.
We agreed to split the bill in half,
that I will choose where we eat next.

Friends Past And

Odeo
with hearts on fire.

I am glad to be reconnected
though our lives have separate ways
gone but now renew in present light
the things we do and how we might
toast the past and still delight each other.

On Another Day

On another day
I might have gone to the bazaar
but today I know you will not be there,
and so I stay home—
besides, it is raining, and I am tired.
Like you, I do not have the energy to be disappointed.

If I go there today in the rain
and you are there,
will you talk to me?
Or will you say not now
you are busy or abruptly
turn away?

The Waves

Waves from your solar plexus
reverberate with mine,
re-enforce and amplify
so strongly I lose balance.

I know not how to shape
this strong connection
and struggle with mere words
to articulate the sound.

I did not learn it at the School
of Internal Weights and Measures;
it is like the wind or, perhaps,
vibrations in the ground.

Solar Perplex-us

The spider web of energy
from my solar plexus
is convulsed in contorted knots
as I try to synthesize emotions.

You asked me why, what, how,
and not to call you back
'til I have something to say.

Remember to breathe.
Then you learn smiling
that will allow laughter. . . .

Sack of Hammers

Like a sack of hammers
we throw our intent
in the direction
of our hopes and dreams

As the sack wobbles
in its unsteady flight,
we watch weight spin
and mass rotate.

We see it fall in the bramble
or clouds of dust;
as we walk to where it lands,
we feel the callous on our hands.

As we approach its resting place,
we see a new horizon,
hear a clearer voice,
pick up the sack
make a better choice,
and hurl the thing
toward a better idea.

THE HORSE KNOWS

Repeating the cycle,
we get there in trust—
we learn what we can
and do what we must.

Sometimes a Poem

Sometimes a poem
can help to mend;
sometimes no rhyme
is at the end.

Sometimes the words
will add no cheer
because of what
we do not hear.

Sometimes the drama
cannot be versed—
any words at all
seem pale or worse.

Sometimes flavors
will go untasted,
and all our spices
will seem wasted.

Sometimes we hurt—
the pain's so much;
it's what we feel
but can not touch.

THE HORSE KNOWS

Sometimes a poem's
no use at all;
though fairly written,
it's just a pall,

A blanket of safety
to protect the child
that resides in us
still, kindling hope.

Sometimes we cut
fingers slicing bread,
consume the sandwich
upon which it bled.

Sometimes the job
we got is lost,
and so we mourn
the letting go.

Sometimes a dad,
while tending tears,
wants his children
to also see joy.

Tender Shoots

Tender shoots want to grow;
they wait for rain—
and so too, thoughts
that are in your brain
wait their turn for you to know.

The Boy, The Fish, The Brahms

With sure-footed confidence, the boy
navigates his way through the adults
crowding the back porch of the amphitheater.

He passes Tom and Marty discussing
their opening remarks to begin
the Symphony's 85th Season.

He passes among musicians mingling
with their instruments prior to the downbeat
as they exchange stories and enthusiasm.

While in the Amp thousands gather expectantly
with attendant books and cushions,
filling it with color and conversation.

He passes the stagehands who,
having completed the pre-concert necessities,
relax around their break table.

All this he observes, but is not distracted.
His mind is steadfast, his steps determined
as he leaves the porch and descends into darkness.
In one hand he carries a fishing pole,
in the other a paper cup of worms.

Oh, the portent! Oh, the joy!
He knows as he walks toward the lake
this will be a special evening;
it's just him, the fish, the Brahms.

The Chair

The Mission-style rocker
was bought at auction
behind a farm house
under a canopy of trees.

I knew the old oak chair
was too large to be comfortable
when I bought it, and yet
it was perfect for rocking three.

Zach on one arm, Becca on the other,
we would rock near the wood stove
as winter clothes dried on the rack,
and watch, out windows, the birds.

Sometimes when reading to them
I might get drowsy or doze
they would say, Daddy, wake up!
Read some more!

Cara read many a book
sitting in it crossed-legged,
or did her homework
while talking on the phone.

And soon, I will rock grandsons
when daughters visit as we celebrate
reunion time, and there I will read to them
from the books so patiently waiting.

The Kitchen

The kitchen smells like garbage;
someone should
take that bag out
and put it in the can.

I wonder,
will the person
who does it
be me?

The Little Bug

The bug in the basin
walked round and round;
though I saw it,
I did not care.
It died with its feet
up in the air.

With a little effort
I might have set it free,
but now its death
is haunting me.

And so it goes—
we ignore the cost
as we consume
and spew exhaust.

The Rivers Run Dry

The rivers run dry in dust.
If you go there, you will catch no fish.
The wells, too, are gone to waste,
the water consumed by corporate corn.

The square lines of man are forgotten
beneath dead soil of tractor ruin
reshaped by nature as a sea of drought
in waves of sand and rubble.

The Snow

The snow that formed 400 miles away
over our farm in Chautauqua County, NY,
is now falling on our house here in NJ.

It happens because the frigid arctic air
crosses the warm Great Lake Erie
and sets up bands of snow that drop
more than 20 feet of snow along
the lake's eastern escarpment.

The snow clouds have mostly evaporated,
but still some have arrived
here over New Jersey
and drop flakes to delight
me as they fall.

There

There
on the bench
where you might have sat
on a warmer day,
the snow accumulates.

It settles as wisps
or drifts lazily
unconcerned,
expressing no hurry in descent.

Occasional sun
melts snow on terracotta roofs,
I hear the drip, drip, drip
during my walk down to town.
I too, do not hurry.

Not far from here,
the overnight snow in the mountains
is measured in feet, while on the valley floor
this dusting will evaporate by noon,
as will these footprints that amuse me.

Later, I will picture you
sitting on that bench
and smile.

This Is Why

This is why.

As I am reupholstering a chair
outside, in the yard dappled sunlight
warms the afternoon;

my bare feet enjoy the grass
someone so considerately planted
fifty years ago;

someone else planted maple trees that
stand seven stories tall, having survived
one hundred and forty winters.

Could the man who made this chair
know with what delight I acknowledge
his craftsmanship as I remove rusty tacks?

All this on my day of rest, with time
to think and do what suits me, employing
so pleasantly my mind, heart, and soul.

As I type out this poem, I see through the
window

THE HORSE KNOWS

the chair awaiting my return
to continue lovingly what was begun.

This is why.

Asked

You asked me what is wrong.
I said I didn't know how to tell it,
the ache is so vague,
but it radiated like fibers
from my solar plexus,

After a few days, when neither
the pain nor vague went away,
I went to the doctor
though he was out of network
and across state lines.

He asked me what was wrong,
I said I didn't know how to tell it
the ache is so vague,
but it radiates like fibers
from my solar plexus.

"Ah," he said, "you need to see
a specialist I know who might
help you to figure out
what these symptoms are about.
Her name is Doctor Flexus."
When I met with her,
it became very clear

THE HORSE KNOWS

she was concerned, and said
she would converse with peers
and sorrow, call me tomorrow.

When the peer review concluded,
she contacted me for an appointment
and arranged a conference,
suggesting I bring a friend or clergy
to meet with her team.

The specialist wore a white coat
with many medals pinned to it,
like a general might wear;
around her neck hung ribbons
with gold medallions.

Reluctantly she told me,
Mr. Swank, you should sit down.
The panel has determined
you have an advanced case
of stage four drama.

It is caused by too much yearning
for purpose or meaning.
You take on the work of others,
and if we had our druthers
you should stop it, so to speak.

She gave to me prescriptions
to reduce my own descriptions
of feelings with so much imagery,
she added, knowingly, I should take
with food, and call her in a week.

You Said

You said,
Embrace the inner child
that is frightened

I thought,
What could I say
that might be interesting?

You embraced yourself,
your arms surrounding your chest,
demonstrating how.

I listened
though you never
looked at me.

You danced
and I danced
but not together.

I thought
on the way home later,
I wish I had spoken.

Dear Friend

Most every day
I look to see
if you are there
where last we met.

I am busy
with lots of work
happy I am able
but miss my art.

How glad to know
our lives transcend
the time and distance
when we're apart.

A Gift In All The World

You teach me to dance
showing in life and art
how to nurture growth
and individuality.

Celebrate what matters.
What we are is not
what we acquire
but rather a gift of life
in all the world
of how we choose to be.

Frost Is/You Matter

Frost is on the rooftop,
snow is on the ridge;
as the dawn is waking,
ice is on the bridge.

You at home are sleeping
I'm awake and see
of all in nature's glory
you matter most to me.

Alarms Will Sound

If you open that door
alarms will sound
especially if
you write it down.

Embracing winds of morning
as dawn awakes,
crows stir the early light
and we breathe deliciously
the air of consciousness
fresh from dreams of night.

As My Son

As my son sails across the ocean
five weeks he will be at sea.
The boat, a 46-foot two-master,
does not seem that big to me.
It would fit inside your store.

How good to share with you
    like family
you who are my friends at Moore's.
And so I say this Thanksgiving,
return home safe and sound to shore,
and when finally comes the new year
we'll celebrate at the hardware store.

Check the Rudder

Check the rudder and the rigging
at 4 a.m. on the overnight watch.
Return to us, my seafaring son,
after 3 years in West Africa.

Catch a fish to bring on board
to eat with your mates
who share not your tongue
but surely your fate.

We will seem much the same,
though you, of course, will not.

The ocean that had been between
now carries you at last toward home.
Let winds be fair and waves be light;
enjoy the sunrise before you sleep.

You left the country of your birth
to find your way a world apart,
and now at last you've come about
to take the tack toward home.

We will seem much the same
though you, of course, will not.

Five weeks to cross as, before the bow,
dolphins play in pressure waves.
The lights at night, shining out,
illuminate the flying fish.

Finally, when you step ashore
and we can all embrace,
we'll celebrate your safe return
and call our friends to feast.

We will seem much the same
though you, of course, will not.

Even In The Dark

Even in the dark, Africa
is hot,
is awake.

People share hunger
outside their huts,
prepare meals
that do not linger,
eating from
the common bowl.

In darkness, we converse
and wait
for the rains to come.

In moonlight
people prepare fields,
repair fences
that are defenses
against the animals
that roam.

Like Dogs

AND YOU . . . how fare you there?
Certainly by now the hay must be in.
If with rain the day begins
walking in, you dry your hair.

Finding still the morning dark
you turn on the lamp to light
the way for pen on paper.
Just as, all dogs must bark,
you write a line
to have your say.

I Have Tools

I am a work in progress
but I have tools and
know how to use them.

As a carpenter
with many years'
experience

I know how to work
under the hood,
under the radar,
under the watchful eye
of doubt,

around corners,
despite the scars
that make me limp.

I am well equipped
to work at night
while I am sleeping.

Even now I am getting
a better idea—
if you are patient,

I can fix me.
I am a carpenter.
I have tools.

At Arms' Length

At arms' length
held apart
we dance
our forms in silhouette
and yet, as art,
we sweep elegantly
matching step for step
each caught in the tension
at arms' length.

What Do I Want?

The trouble is,
I don't need much.
As I grew up
the standard was,
What do we need?
So if I don't need anything
nothing's on the need list.

Then the follow up is,
What do I want?
This begins to sound like excess,
starts to prick
my cautious conscience.

Thank you, daughter,
for helping me articulate
so now we both can understand.

I Watch You

I watch you
from the restaurant window
(I hope you do not mind)
while you and your mom
eat dinner and watch the sun
setting, obscured by clouds
gray like the Great Lake.

Beneath The Snow Wait Seeds

There dispersed by
winds of fall,
beneath the snow wait seeds
to soon renew, begin the growth of roots
that heal the cut called furrow.

Bloom where you are planted.
Never regret locale.
With emotion take a chance.
Nurture both the root and dream
and let your body dance.

The Horse Knows

Up the hill near the barn
across one hundred yards of grass,
the horse knows
when I stop along the road
to take his photo.
In recognition
he turns to face the lens
of my camera, my intent.

While I photograph,
he barely moves
steadfast in his gaze,
planted in his stance
ears pitched forward inquiringly;
in unwavering focus
we acknowledge our mutual
curiosity and sentience.

Across our nostrils
blow pre-storm breezes,
we hear bustle in the barn,
we hear rumbling
clouds encroaching,
feel the warmth
of swirling grasses,
the consciousness we share.

How It Comes About

Like the man who sets the sail,
I pull the paper taut and tack—
precise, deliberate, against the wind,
sail words across the page
toward you.

Rebecca A.

Dearest Rebecca,
I am glad these things
are well with you.

If you read between
the lines or try,
you will know I
am about to cry.

Love,
Dad

Do You Know?

Do you know
each word here spoken
drips like blood
and will stain the carpet?

Do you know
connecting the drops
like dots make pictures
as a child might draw?

Do you know
these lines can conjure
prehistoric images
found in the caves of France?

Do you know
this simplistic art
of quill on parchment
is not written with a pen?

Do you know
the emotions here spit
crunch like seeds
from an apple?

THE HORSE KNOWS

Do you know
these words are not
as I imagine
my own blood?

Do you know
I will not die
if you forget this poem
my face, my name?

Do you know
like the birds
we must 'til death
sing out our songs?

Do you know
how good it feels
to share this space,
this time, with you?

Mom Comes Home

After years of living away,
Mom is returning to live with me
in the family farm house built in 1838.
She calls, she is crying
she wants to come home—
please, please, could I bring her home?
I fly to get her.
We rent a truck, we pack, I drive.
She holds the cat on her lap.
She sings.

Since the stroke,
we help her stand;
she goes slow
in the walker.
She wants to die
here at home.
You think moving is easy?
You think this is fun?

Still she taps her foot to music,
still her eyes can twinkle,
still her face can smile.
My sister now cares for her,
opens the shutters to the morning light.

THE HORSE KNOWS

When Laurie asks if that's alright,
Mom blinks her eyes to mean yes.

Again we gather this Thanksgiving
to share with her our love;
still she eats the ice cream cone,
still she whispers, Wonderful,
still she sings her song.

Finding

Finding the bright of each day
is looking and
being curious, expectant,
ready to be delighted. . .
what a wonderful way to savor the present,
the sights and sounds of smell and emotion,
the touch of life.

Mom is listening to swing music at the moment
we try to keep her toe. . .a-tappin'

She sends me this mental note:
We are fine really. . .we know the physical is
not our true identity.

She sends joy
clear and simple,
blue sky after rain.

Each Morning Now She Sits

Each morning now she sits
on her bed at the foot
with hands along the wall to find
still she is alive and
wonders why aloud to me.

She tries to do it right,
saying in her prayers each night,
God, I'm ready to be with thee—
help me cross over
or give me back my sight
to see my children
who care for me.

Mom Is Angry

Is it a cry out of pain
or something else
that she does, remaining
stuck in our world,
when she wants to go?
Which is it? How can we know?
We all want for her that which is good;
that she finds peace
we wish she could.
Is it the physical—
is that what we see?
She does not need it
any more.
Her real self
has traveled to the beyond;
she no longer lives
in her shell.

Bait on the Hook

I've got bait on a hook
but every time I look
no fish is in sight.
I would be so glad
if only I had
a serious bite,
and there to begin
to reel you in.

Becca About Her Beau

We laugh
because he is kind,
because I feel secure and whole
when we are together—
I am free to be me. . .with him.

We laugh because we can,
because we know he cares
enough to be sure
before he speaks
what he wants to say.

He is my counterbalance
and lets me take the chance
to hope, to dream, to discover
how I want to dance.

Fixing

Do you think when we are old
our kids will scream and shout
because I filled the barn with stuff
that they must now throw out?

What where you thinking?
will they ask, when you filled the barn,
piling there the furniture
to repair or save from harm?

Was it neglect or circumstance
that caused the abandoned dreams
to be curbside? Do you bring them home
just because you have the means?

All that, I know is true,
but still I hope I might
someday repair them all
and thus have peace at night.

Fixing for me is a primal need—
call me the doc of things;
let me figure out the how
with all the joy that brings.

Elsewhere

Everywhere
the blossoms bloom,
life will find us
if there's room.

You do not answer
when I phone
or else explain
you're not alone.

Another time
perhaps is better—
when it's cold
I wear a sweater.

Expect Sum Net Experiential Zen

Net sum learning by:
At least once, I
gave it a try.

Surviving my successes and failures...mostly
Milking cows,
Hunting with a bow,
Burning legs rolling hot steel at the mill,
Flipping a car at 50 mph,
Burying a car by the baseball diamond,
Surviving a deadly disease,
Playing with fire,
Hoping to goodness,
Freezing my fingers,
Teaching in a foreign land,
Being recognized as a master puppeteer,
Performing for a million people,
Helping raise 3 great kids,
Running a business at age 15
Painting houses
Doing plumbing and electrical work,
Spending the night in a freezer,
Riding a bicycle 140 miles in a day
    of 90-degree heat,
Falling asleep while riding a bicycle,

Going winter tent-camping,
Dropping the flashlight
   butt down the latrine,
Hiking mountains in New Mexico,
Hitchhiking around the United States,
Being reported missing,
Being reported dead,
Becoming an artist and poet,
Loving an awesome woman,
Being applauded by patrons and staff
   of a nail salon,
Holding a live hummingbird in the hand,
Walking into the windy rain of a Nor'easter,
Flying in a glider,
Damming a creek,
Firing guns,
Playing an instrument,
Falling off a horse,
Hanging by the heels,
Building tree houses,
Clinging to the upper reaches of a tree
   in a fierce wind storm,
Stopping cars with a single snowball,
Nearly drowning,
Being tear-gassed as a child,
Protecting wild creatures from certain death,
Communicating with birds,

THE HORSE KNOWS

Designing and building the house,
Crewing on a 16th-century merchant ship,
Being hit with a cast iron fry pan,
Saving a man's life twice in the same hour,
Wrestling to a draw father and son,
Sleeping in a cornfield overnight,
Receiving a postcard from Isaac Asimov,
Loading semi-trailer trucks,
Working in vineyards,
Exploring caves,
Chasing a bull with my son,
Sitting with children on the peak of the roof,
Getting stung by hornets, wasps, and bees,
Being hit in the head by a falling acorn,
Kicking out streetlights,
Being sheltered by strangers,
Watching the archeologist dance,
Directing a musical,
Living among the Amish
Helping raise their barns,
Writing poetry in a Polynesian hut,
Processing my share of snot,
Chasing chickens for pay,
Giving blood too slowly,
Doing something for shits and grins,
Being knocked loopy,
Being taken away in an ambulance,

Shoveling snow off rooftops,
Climbing down buildings,
Being hosted by a Savannah Belle,
Eating dinner with a cinematographer,
Making bad assumptions and good
   decisions,
Retrieving something from the toilet,
Being congratulated by a movie star,
Planting vegetables,
Teaching a child to ride a bike,
Doing a walk-on part for a Mexican theater,
Inviting Lou to be in the art show,
Building a 14' Banks Dory,
Dismantling a building with a Chevy drive
   shaft,
Handing a diva some toilet paper,
Saving the barn from a brush fire,
Taking a nap while flying a kite,
Getting a better idea,
Forming an artist consortium,
Donating the profits to the library,
Being the honored guest,
Holding his head in my lap as he breathes his last,
Bartering poetry for pie,
Knowing which way is north.

From each event what did I learn?

THE HORSE KNOWS

Experience shapes but not defines;
whatever we do, our net sum climbs.
I've done a list; it's now your turn.

Our New Mayor

He used to be just the guy at Moore's,
which of course is our best store,
explaining what, the why, the for;
now he serves *hors d'ouevres*,
meeting with his fellow mayors.

We hope that he's our best mayor yet
while munching down the *Crêpes Suzette*.
We like his style 'til he forgets
on whom it was we placed our bets

If he gets too big for his own britches,
we'll go out back and get some switches;
we'll storm his office, of course, which is
bound to give him facial twitches—
but 'til then, we send well wishes
while he helps the wife do the dishes.

Hear The Hum

Hear the hum,
and too
may good be expressed
in lives so present
that life has wings.

And yet
the warmth of memories
gives to each
stability
a depth of soul
that helps the present
to resound.

Why are you gone
mad and packing?
Just some stuff
I hope you say,
or is it so
you move away?

And if it is, and must be so
then travel well, I hope you know.
Peace for you is my intent;
if you find it along the road
my wish has been well spent.

How Good

How good to know that birds can fly;
how good to know that you and I,
stretching wings, hop and dance—
how glad to be when, if by chance
we ever meet, replete with words,
we'll soar, like fellow birds.

How

How, when you finally speak
the words waiting
within your voice,
you articulate a heart
so profoundly full—
like tapestries
from foreign lands.

When all the world
becomes at last
familiar as the place called home
where heart, mind, and soul
can do the hard and necessary
work of coagulation,
you express truths
by how you place
the words you choose.

It is for each of us the same
if we chance to have our say
beyond the small provincial realm,
we dare to share essential selves
with travelers along the way.

I Bought Your Book

I bought your book
and like a curse
I read it all,
verse by verse.

I dragged my mind
across each page,
spoke each word
inside your cage,

Gleaned the import
from the drivel
around each corner
joint and swivel.

Your rhyme and meter
were never flawed
you even spelled right
woppy jawed

which means of course
amiss, askew,
and other words
that, if I knew
what they meant

THE HORSE KNOWS

I'd give them
up for Lent.

I deduced the context
by luck and hunches,
read them twice
again in bunches,
just stopping to piss
and eat my lunches.

Tossed among your humor, wit
against my will, and bit by bit
I began to like your writing style
wearing your shoes too big to fit
I felt your pain, walked your mile.
Finally, I see from where you sit
though it took a little while.

You are a man who tells a tale
like the proverbial check
that's in the mail;
I read on, uncrooked my neck.

You do not quit
'til all is sorted out,
convince with mirth
contrary to my moaning.

Beyond a doubt, the book's
so very worth my owning.

I Live Among Dragons

I live among dragons
who breathe with smoke
and snort with blasts
of flames that turn to ashes
the garden I call dreams.

In Italy

In Italy, if you muse
it is in Italian
and narrow shoes.

On a cobblestone street,
maybe you will choose
a good *ristorante*!

Pencil Lead

The coffee tastes like pencil lead.
Was it something that I said?

City of Changes

There is a spring of fresh water
that flows in the City of Changes
toward which I sail
across a clamorous sea.

The unsettling winds of anomie
stretch the rigging lines and sails
to the edge of their tensile strength.
I would change my hair for you.

You Surely Have

You surely have tied me in knots
with bowlines and half hitches
of lines that hold fast sailing ships—
and with slender thread and stitches.

Little Bird

Your song once unfamiliar,
unknown though surely sweet,
amazes me with delight—
how it swells my heart!

There among my lists and plans
you sit to sun your outstretched wings;
your hop and chirp awaken me;
with ease and grace you pour your song.

Love Magic

Love magic happens.
It is like the tide:
We need but to let it
wash over us. . .
feel the ebb and flow.

Love happens without us
needing to control everything.
Our part is to be ready,
to witness and acknowledge.

We must let love breathe.

Do not try to contain the ocean
in a small conceptual cup.

Predator Drones

Now that we
have tested
the predator drones
in foreign countries,
proving that they
can also kill civilians,
they can be safely used
to kill people
here in the Americas.

This Poem

This poem has been hermetically sealed.
It contains alliteration but no rhymes,
illusions, or unreasonable hopes

No references to Homer, Dionysus,
guacamole, Shakespeare, or Blake,
nor our crumbling infrastructure.

It does not comment
about failed policies, politics,
or the continued destruction
of nature and whole populations
by corporate greed and those who operate
the machinery of plunder and acquisition.

This poem is about
a father who takes his children
to find pussy willows and polliwogs
living in the ruined basement
of a house long ago destroyed by fire,
its foundation filled by a spring flowing
near a stand of tall pine trees where
raucous crows cavort and clamor.

The Map Is Not The Territory

The day is Thursday.
The day is very warm for November.
As I leave the hardware store, the sun is shining intensely on my face and arms. Walking past the storefronts toward the corner where I will turn up the side street, I notice, ahead of me, the Korean beauty salon door is propped open to let in the fresh air. I am thinking, how wonderfully appropriate this is when, suddenly, a sparrow flies past me and through the doorway into the salon. "Wow," I say as I walk past the door and turn the corner to go up the side street. But then I stop.

Through the glass window on this side of the shop, I watch the bird fly inside over the heads of the startled stylists and patrons. They duck their heads and wave arms amusingly. Soon the bird flees the rear of the shop, swoops in my direction, and —*smack*—hits the inside of the window. In that moment we are nose to beak. We are both stunned. The frustrated bird settles on a window display and looks at me.

In his autobiography *The Man who Listens to Horses*, Monty Roberts suggests that, when we want to communicate with another species, we do so in mental pictures. I picture the bird turning and flying out the door. I see my right arm rising and hand pointing through the glass toward the door. I hear my voice saying, "Just fly out the door." The bird immediately turns and does so.

Interesting, I am thinking and, turning to go, notice the people inside have watched the bird and me interact. They seem transfixed. Then, as they awake to the present, our eyes meet. I smile sheepishly and give a little shrug. They smile and applaud politely.

I walk home thinking, The salon people are happy. The bird is happy. I am happy.

Busted Things

Things busted, broken, trashed,
things dimpled, dinged, and dashed,
things crumpled, rumpled, crashed,
or mangled, mungled, mashed—

yup, I fix with good intent and care,
be they table, bed, or chair.

People Like You

I am thinking,
as the rain swirls
across my front door,
how swell it is
to know people like you.

I hope the weather there is fair,
that you do not wilt in the heat,
that you find time to put up your feet
as you sip the evening air.

Thoughts

1.

Our thoughts are like rocks—
some pebbles,
some boulders.
They may be stood upon
to gain vision
or they may be dropped on people.

Mostly we drop them.

2.

We are the 99% that
let our government drop them
all over the planet
as corporate vouchers
and smart bombs
that kill equally well
the just and the unjust,
the foe and the friend
especially the innocent.

We allow the systems to be created
that suppress our opportunity,

systems that fail education,
employment, health care.
We further diminish opportunity
by incarcerating by the millions
into private prisons that insure
access to wealth, mobility, or power is nil.

Thus we and our children
are indentured to a system
of corporate manipulation,
fees and debt payments,
that make the keepers rich,
but the people poor.

Today Is

Today is one of those days
I do not feel clever or witty
or bright,
just trying to remember
what needs doing and
getting that much right.

Today let the rains
wash away the tears.
I am just a man
doing the laundry,
hanging some sadness
on the line to dry,
waiting for the sun.

My Daughter Says

My daughter says
there is a polliwog
in the pond,
a little tyke
swimming round,
and, gee, what glee
she is telling me.

Well Intentioned, But

Thank you for correcting me,
I respond

when you say,
Don't try to help!

What When Walking We

What do we notice,
when we are out walking
among the nature sounds,
if we are lost in conversation
like nurses making rounds?

What do I feel
when we are at the gallery
as you praise the modern art
while I strive to master
the subtle, public fart?

What is the taste,
as my hand holds cup, in a haste
I pour creamer that I found
and wait the hot black slurry waste
to drain from coffee grounds?

Three Sides of the Circle

Three sides of the circle.
What is it?
A poem?
A short story?
An Escher-like drawing?
Does it make a sound?
Does it walk like a cat?

Three sides of a circle—
what is that?

Poetry Suite

1. Who Are You

Who are you that figures so profoundly,
knowing from where each breath will come,
who commands the waves of my distant ocean
to rise and fall like an unseen moon?

Who are you, so unknown, that demands
account of why I dream or cry,
who compels me in silence to speak
in answers taken down from hangers
and wear the dreams there hung so long?

Who are you that knows, not just the from,
but the where of going too,
weaving days of dawn through dusk
into night seas of pastel stars?
So much a Flavian princess you,
fairly soon now, will I know who?

2. You Who Are

You who are the one it seems
appearing nightly in my dreams
vigorous, delightful, with lyric smile

a symphony so sophisticated
my breath forever is abated.

Mozart, Bartok, and Beethoven
were they beside me now,
staring at you with mouths agape
would whisper, Wow. And as
we at each other sideways glance,
going then our separate ways,
I'm hoping there's at least a chance
to meet this cello woman
and find with flaw or not,
at last kiss you who are so hot.

3. *Who Could Expect You*

Who could expect the stars
to line up in parade
with flags unfurled, in flying art
to march right down my street
and penetrate my heart?

Who could expect or know
that all the tears I, silent, shed
like waves that wash ashore,
each with new adventures, would
come to splash against my door?

THE HORSE KNOWS

Who could expect the songs
of birds that sing, bring the dawn
to awaken me, the same,
would, so clear and in my tongue,
be calling out my name?

Who could expect the beauty you
in all the world might find and pick
from the heap of broken charms,
the man, the youth, the child, me
to welcome into your loving arms?

Why Men Never

Men never say, I told you so,
because men never think of it first.

It never occurs to them—
only now are they realizing
what the wife knew last week,
and what she has since
reconsidered, reworked,
adjusted, and revised
taken to the lawyer,
had notarized,
and written a humorous
article about
for the *New York Times*,
which appeared Sunday
in the magazine section.

Before The Sun Is Up

I am up before the sun.

Overnight my brain
has figured out the flaws
of my previous day;
will this helpful knowledge
lead to solutions?

I wonder how today
will allow me to employ
with skill the better ideas
that are needed.

You Sparkle

I
find
a
sparkling
stone
and
think
of
you.

In the Company of Angels

Fly each day
in the company of angels,
the joy of understanding,
in the presence of peace.

Express your joy of life,
ability to see,
your sense of self.

Your willingness to love
(if I can use that word)
will light your way
along paths unseen.

STEVEN SWANK

I Am

I am in a mess;
there is no telling
how to fix it.

Will there be yelling?

White Fluff

White fluff is on the ground
as I type on Grandma's breadboard—
great rye bread she'd make;
what a treat to know
I can share with you the taste.

My Heart Is

My heart is addicted to the sun,
and now it is going down.
I notice the change in energy. . .
the sense of loss leaves a mark.

I know the Earth goes around,
that the sun also rises;
still, I count on you, it's true,
to be a candle in my dark.

Kite Tied to Toe

I hope you are well
and have a place to hunker up
during the high water. . .
do you think
if I sleep with a kite tied to my toe
it is necessary to also
be wearing a life jacket?

Puzzling It Out

Good to hear you
puzzling life out:
Sometimes the pieces fit
in unexpected ways.

We sometimes see the fit
at least a bit,
and sometimes they won't—
even though we press,
they don't.

He Says, She Says

He says, "What time do we need to be at the Hendersons' for dinner?"

She says, "Sweetheart, could you check the curried yams in the oven in about 15 minutes while I go to rehearsal? And oh, cut some irises to take with us for the table, I promised Beverly we would. The flowers will match the tablecloth, the one we loaned to them for their 30th anniversary two years ago, the one with the wine stain that your brother Fred made when he stayed with us that January."

He says, "What time do we need to leave?"

She says, "If you could get some fresh fruit for the salad and cut it up, but not so big like you usually do, and use the blue bowl from my sister that she found at the yard sale when they lived in Virginia on that cul-de-sac that they hated so much even though they had their own driveway. Remember? She gave us the bowl when we stayed with them, and as we were leaving you backed the car over their neighbor's dog while it was still on the leash. The neighbors were so mad! And I can understand why, seeing the leash just disappear under the car like that. Really, it could happen to anyone."

He says, "What time should I be dressed and ready?"

She says, "You don't need to be fancy dressed, just wear something nicer than what you wore last time.

Maybe the sweater Joe Muzio gave you before they sold their house and moved to Massachusetts. Have you heard anything from them since they moved last year? And a nice belt—your black one, it will match your good shoes. And promise me, if you're going to town, don't stop at the Emmerling's today. Edna said Bill has just gotten a hair transplant, and he is in a *foul* mood. You know how he is when he gets like that. . . . Might he be the one who has your power saw? You should write down who you lend your tools to. That way, when you need them, you could look at your list."

He says nothing, but he is thinking something.

She says from the other room, "What?"

He walks into the foyer, where she is preparing to leave, gives her a kiss, and tells her he loves her endearing ways. He holds open the door for her.

As she drives away, she calls out her open window, "Please be ready on time." He smiles and waves.

A Vigil In Snow

A vigil in snow
that clings to clothing
is a principled stand
against the wind
of oppression—

a vigil in snow
with peace in mind
where men with guns
wait and watch
your breath condense.

A vigil in snow:
I image you warm,
safe with friends
who share with you
the journey for change.

I send angels
to counsel, protect,
inspire the joy
that freedom brings
while expressing life.

I love
who you are,

what you do,
as what we do
is who we are.

But Words

These past few days
I have been trying
to find words
that might comfort
but words fail

If I were there
I would hold you
we would cry and
scream the anguish
injustice brings

I send my love
that is not enough,
too far away, incomplete,
to make things right
or remove the pain

I send waves and beams
of energy to support your day
and what you must do
to find your path
through the disarray

I am mindful these words
are pale representatives

of my hopes for you
to find your balance
and laugh again.

Bring the Light

Bring the light with you this morning
into the dark court,
shine with passion and truth,
protect the youth
from the oppressive weight
of laws so carefully employed
to keep humble the masses.

We Eat

We who live in western NY State
eat disappointment and loss
for breakfast, then go to work.

The sky is overcast October through May
preventing the light, a perpetual gray,
from reaching our soul or touching our pain.

Thus we prepare for the harshness of winter,
twenty feet of snow, temperatures near zero
or even below.

It Is Not

It is not easy to iron a fish
or keep soap in a broken dish
undo the wrong of being mean
that cause the tears
in a child's dream.

Like Elephants

Like elephants
who greet each other with trumpets,
flapping ears, snorts, and gushes. . . .
so we greet each other
and, too, applaud the dawn.

Life On The High Wire

Like those who on the wire dance,
we are suspended on beliefs.
Intent draws taut as if by chance
Life's dimensional relief.

Entity fibers bound by light
illuminate the scenes,
while on the wire in the night
we spin dizzily the dreams.

The Tension

It is the tension of the string
that is my delight

It is the tension of the wind
that flies the kite

Whether handmade by Grandpa
or bought at the store

Boxes and diamonds
and dragons are more

Than pieces of fabric
out on a string.

Then tension is magic
and tension's the thing

I love most about flying
when out with a kite

Like the magic and tension,
when kissing good night.

Index of Titles

A Gift In All The World, *53*
A Vigil In Snow, *127*
Alarms Will Sound, *55*
Amish/English, *5*
As A Poet, *1*
As I Walk and Breathe, *14*
As My Son, *56*
Asked, *48*
At Arms' Length, *63*
Bait on the Hook, *77*
Becca About Her Beau, *78*
Before The Sun Is Up, *117*
Beneath The Snow Wait Seeds, *66*
Bring the Light, *131*
Busted Things, *104*
But Words, *129*
Chance For Walt, *2*
Check the Rudder, *57*
City of Changes, *96*
Dear Friend, *52*
Do You Know?, *70*
Drumming, *9*
Each Morning Now She Sits, *75*
Editor, *11*
Elsewhere, *80*
Even In The Dark, *59*
Expect Sum Net Experiential Zen, *81*
Finding, *74*

Fingers/Hands, *10*
Five-Inch Rain, *13*
Fixing, *79*
Friends Past And, *28*
Frost Is/You Matter, *54*
He Says, She Says, *125*
Hear The Hum, *87*
How, *89*
How Good, *88*
How It Comes About, *68*
I Am, *120*
I Am Drawn, *16*
I Bought Your Book, *90*
I Have Tools, *61*
I Hoped, *15*
I Watch You, *65*
In Italy, *94*
In The Attic, *17*
In the Company of Angels, *119*
Ironing A Fish, *20*
It Is Not, *133*
It's Just Math, *21*
Kite Tied to Toe, *123*
Life On The High Wire, *135*
Like Dogs, *60*
Like Elephants, *134*
Like Icarus, *23*
Little Bird, *98*
Love Magic, *99*
Maybe Today, *24*
Men, *19*

Mom Comes Home, *72*
Mom Is Angry, *76*
My Daughter Says, *109*
My Fear, *25*
My Heart Is, *122*
My Son Eats Fish, *26*
On Another Day, *29*
Our New Mayor, *86*
Pencil Lead, *95*
People Like You, *105*
Poetry Suite, *113*
Predator Drones, *100*
Puzzling It Out, *124*
Rebecca A., *69*
Sack of Hammers, *32*
Solar Perplex-us, *31*
Sometimes a Poem, *34*
Tender Shoots, *36*
The Boy, The Fish, The Brahms, *37*
The Chair, *39*
The Horse Knows, *67*
The Kitchen, *41*
The Little Bug, *42*
The Map Is Not The Territory, *102*
The Rivers Run Dry, *43*
The Snow, *44*
The Tension, *136*
The Waves, *30*
There, *45*
These Little Poems, *4*
This Is Why, *46*

This Little Poem, *3*
This Poem, *101*
Thoughts, *106*
Three Sides of the Circle, *112*
Today Is, *108*
We Eat, *132*
Well Intentioned, But, *110*
What Do I Want?, *64*
What When Walking We, *111*
White Fluff, *121*
Why Men Never, *116*
You Must, *8*
You Said, *51*
You Sparkle, *118*
You Surely Have, *97*

www.ingramcontent.com/pod-product-compliance
Lightning Source LLC
LaVergne TN
LVHW091300080426
835510LV00007B/333